HIGHLIGHTS
CANBERRA
A Pictorial Journey

HIGHLIGHTS
CANBERRA

A Pictorial Journey

Above and left: Canberra, in the heart of the ACT

Pages 6-9: Old Parliament House was officially opened in 1927 and was replaced by the new building, opened in 1988

Above: The Lodge is the official residence of the Australian Prime Minister in Canberra

Right: Old Parliament House

Above and right: The meeting place of the nation, Parliament House is the pinacle of Capital Hill and has a 81-metre flagpole

This page: The Senate sits in maroon chambers

Previous page: The view from Parliament House

The Australian House of Representatives, where the Prime Minister and Leader of the oposition are based

The main foyer of Parliament House

Above and right: Anzac Parade

Above: Anzac statue

Left: A military ceremony on Anzac Parade

Above and right: International Flags at the High Court of Australia

Above: The changing colours of autumn

Left: Government House, Yarralumla, is residence to the Queen's representative, the Governor-General

Above: Autumn leaves

Left: The National Library of Australia

Above: Black Mountain Tower (formerly Telstra Tower)

Right: Parkes Place and Black Mountain Tower in the background

Previous page: National Film and Sound Archive

The Australian National Botanic Gardens showcase a vast collection of Australian flora and fauna

This page and following page: The Australian National Botanic Gardens were officially opened in October of 1970

Shoppers take advantage of Canberra's cafe culture

Above: Contemporary sculpture, National Gallery of Australia

Right: The High Court of Australia is nestled next to
Lake Burley Griffin

Above and left: Once an administrative building, the heritage-listed John Gorton Building is now home to the Australian Department of Environment and Heritage

The Australian Institute of Sport is a world class
centre for elite athletes

Over 1 million people visit the Australian Institute of Sport
each year

Above: Minature trains passing at Cockington Green

Left: Built in 1860, Blundell's Cottage pre-dates Canberra

51

Above and right: Since 1979 models at Cockington Green have grown from quaint English villages to international displays

The cricket pitch at Cockington Green is a favourite amongst tourists and locals

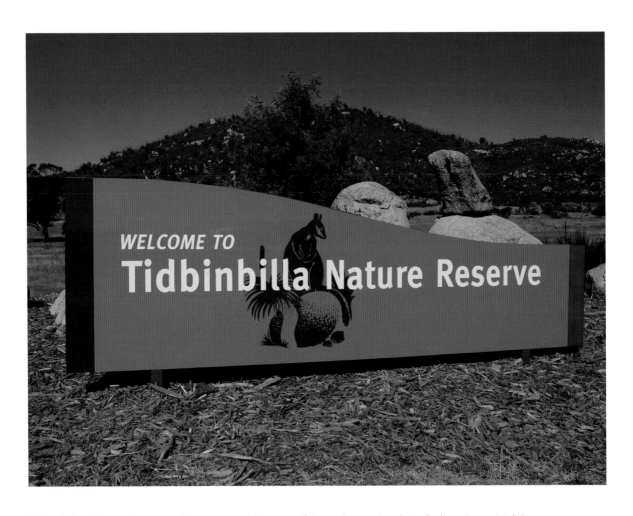

Tidbinbilla Nature Reserve is home to a collection of Australian animals including Emus (right)

Above: Deciduous trees line Canberra streets

Right: Ginninderra Village

Gold Creek Village demonstrates the life of
Australian pioneer settlements

Above and right: The Australian Reptile Centre is home to all things reptillian

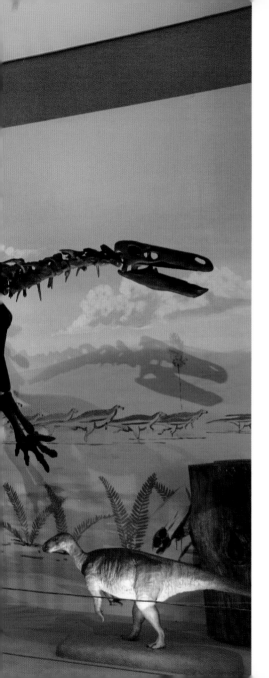

Prehistoric fossils come to life at the
National Dinosaur Museum

The Australian War Memorial is a monument to Australian military history

The Australian War Memorial houses a vast collection of models,
dioramas and military archives

Above: Scrivener Dam was built to withstand once in 5000 year floods
Right: Aerial view of Lake Burley Griffin and surrounds

Above: The Australian National University is the only Australian university established by an Act of Federal Parliament
Left: Lake Burley Griffin

Questacon; The National Science and Technology Centre displays more than 200 interactive exhibits

The current Questacon building was a gift from Japan for Australia's Bicentenary in 1988

Sculptures line the parkland surrounding Questacon

The seasonal leaves of Parkes Place make it a scenic pathway year-round

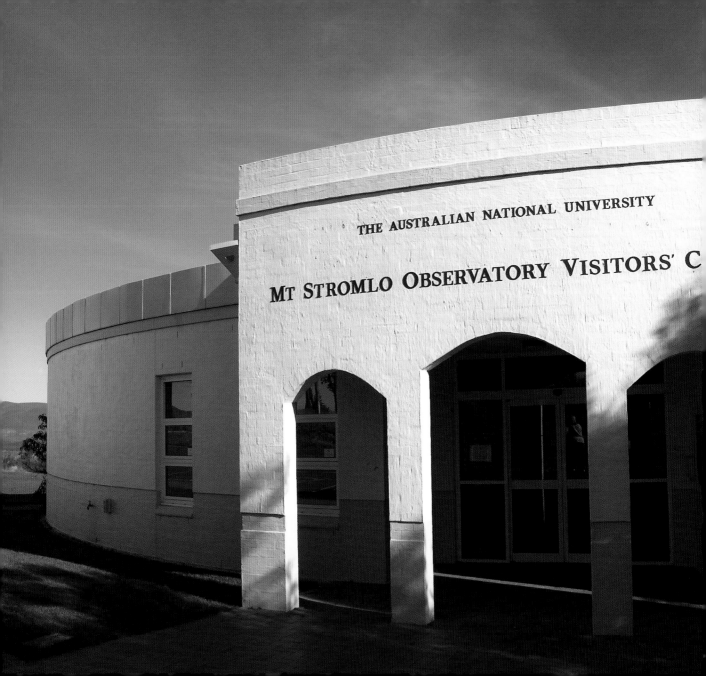

Above and left: Mount Stromlo Observatory is Australia's premier centre for astronomical research

Above and right: The Shine Dome is the first building in Canberra to be included on the National Heritage List and has received numerous awards since its opening in 1959

Above: A civic statue

Left: The patternered surface of the National Museum of
Australia includes words written in Braille

Above: The brightly coloured loop featured outside the National Museum of Australia is an installation that forms part of the Uluru Line, which reaches across Acton Peninsula

Right: An aerial view of the National Museum of Australia and the Acton Peninsula

Situated at the approximate centre of Canberra, Lake Burley
Griffin is named after Walter Burley Griffin, the city's architect

Above and right: Canberra Deep Space Centre

Above: The National Observatory and Planetarium, a landmark in Canberra, but with an uncertain future

Above: As part of the National Museum this free form sculpture reflects the Australian landscape, with Black Mountain Tower in the distance

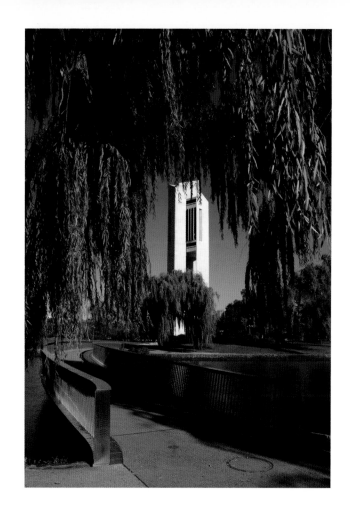

Above: The bridge to Aspen Island and the National Carillon
Left: Lake Burley Griffin and the National Carillon. A gift from the British Government to the Australian people, it has 55 bells

Above: Autumn colour at Reserve
Right: Lake Burley Griffin is a favorite for picnickers

First published in Australia in 2008 by
New Holland Publishers (Australia) Pty Ltd
Sydney • Auckland • London • Cape Town

1/66 Gibbes Street Chatswood NSW 2067 Australia
218 Lake Road Northcote Auckland New Zealand
86 Edgware Road London W2 2EA United Kingdom
80 McKenzie Street Cape Town 8001 South Africa

National Library of Australia Cataloguing-in-Publication entry

Canberra.

ISBN: 9781741106862 (hbk.)

Highlight series

Canberra (A.C.T.)--Pictorial works.

919.471

Publisher: Fiona Schultz
Publishing Manager: Lliane Clarke
Designer: Natasha Hayles
Photographer: Graeme Gillies
Production Manager: Linda Bottari
Printer: SNP Leefung

10 9 8 7 6 5 4 3 2 1